NEWCASTLE UPON~TYNE

A 1914 Sketchbook
Robert J. S. Bertram

NEWCASTLE UPON~TYNE

A 1914 Sketchbook by
Robert J.S. Bertram

Spredden Press
Stocksfield 1990

First published by A. & C. Black, 1914.
Reprinted 1916.
Reprinted 1990, by
The Spredden Press
Brocksbushes Farm
Stocksfield
Northumberland NE45 7WB

© Helen Joyce Swain and
Charles Neville Bertram

ISBN 1 871739 07 1

Printed and bound by
Smith Settle, Otley,
West Yorkshire LS21 3JP

Robert J.S. Bertram

Robert John Scott Bertram (1871-1953) was an artist who worked all his life in the north, recording landscape and historical buildings in watercolour, oil and pen and ink and pencil sketches. He is probably best known now for his delightful drawings of the traditional buildings of the county for several of the volumes of the *Northumberland County History.* He was much in demand for illustrating books which included guides to the East and North Ridings of Yorkshire and Northumberland, *A Fisher's Garland* by John Harbottle, William Sitwell's *The Border,* Howard Pease's *Northumbrian Decameron* and Sir Arthur Middleton's *Account of Belsay Castle.*

Shortly before the outbreak of the 1914-18 war he was commissioned by the publishers A. & C. Black to make sketch books of four historic cities: Durham, Newcastle, York and Chester but, because of the war, only the Newcastle and Durham sketches were published. The pencil drawings, which show a mastery of this medium, have great vitality and charm. They show the cities as they were at the turn of the century with steam trains, trams and buildings now altered or destroyed. There are some outstanding sketches of the interior of Durham cathedral, for Bertram was also an excellent architectural draftsman.

He was passionately interested in the preservation of the historical buildings of Newcastle and was, for many years, secretary of the Bishop's Advisory Committee for the care of churches. Historically, his main interest was Newcastle in the eighteenth century and he painted a lunette for the Laing Art Gallery, Newcastle, showing 'The River Tyne during the great flood of 1771'.

Bertram was born in Newcastle, the son of a ship's chandler, and at the age of fourteen was apprenticed in a shipping office. His talent was evident at an early age and he won a scholarship to the Durham College of Science, Newcastle, where he later became a teacher, at first combining his teaching with work for a cabinet maker and interior designer. In his early years he was influenced by William Morris in the field of design and by J.M.W. Turner in landscape composition but an individual style soon emerged.

In 1920 he came Master of Design at Armstrong College (later King's College and now Newcastle University) and he kept this position until his retirement in 1938 when he moved from Corbridge, where he had built himself a house, to Whitby. There he continued to work until his death.

James Alder, artist and former student of Bertram, writes: 'He was a man of boundless energy, an inspiring teacher with a deep interest of nature. At the age of thirteen my own interests in art were forever confirmed when I first met this irrepressible man. Showing me a collection of beautiful drawings of blackberries he said: "No, there is not one kind but hundreds of varieties, if you will look into their design. Nature is always experimenting." To those who know them, his pencil drawings are a joy. Always rich in texture, they show in their clever placing of blacks, greys and white a grasp of that elusive quality that Thomas Bewick called "colour". In the use of the simple pencil, strangely known to old-fashioned Geordies as a "vine", he shows himself to be a superb craftsman.'

NEWCASTLE·FROM·GATESHEAD

THE·SOUTH·POSTERN.

THE·BLACKGATE

THE·GREAT·HALL·OF·THE·CASTLE.

THE·SALLYPORT.

THE · CATHEDRAL:
from Groat·Market

ST·NICHOLAS'·AND·THE·BLACK·GATE·FROM·THE·CASTLE

SAINT ANDREW'S CHURCH

SAINT·JOHNS·CHURCH

CHAPEL·IN·THE·TRINITY·HOUSE

ALL·SAINTS·CHURCH

ST. MARYS CHURCH: GATESHEAD.

HOLY JESUS HOSPITAL

SURTEES' HOUSE; SANDHILL

GREY·STREET

BLACKETT·STREET

NEVILLE STREET

THE QUAYSIDE.

THE·FOUR·BRIDGES

ELSWICK·WORKS.

PALMERS' JARROW.

HIGH·AND·LOW·LIGHTS·NORTH·SHIELDS

IN·JESMOND·DENE.